FROM THE
HEART
— OF A —
WARRIOR

An Inspirational Chronicle
of Poems for the Soul

MENDEZ FRITH

ISBN: 979-8-9881484-1-8 (Paperback)
ISBN: 979-8-9881484-0-1 (Hardback)
ISBN: 979-8-9881484-2-5 (eBook)
Library of Congress Control Number: 2023907118

Book design by Dara Publishing
Printed in the United States of America.

Disclaimer: The publisher and the authors do not make any guarantee or other promise as to any results that may be obtained from using the content of this book. This publication is meant as a source of valuable information for the reader, however it is not meant as a substitute for direct expert assistance. If such level of assistance is required, the services of a competent professional should be sought.

Dedication

To my family… past, present and future.

Contents

❝

It is important that when we make a resolution, or establish a goal, that we take the ACTION necessary to accomplish that goal.
Steve Maraboli

❞

Note From Author

From the Heart of a Warrior: An Inspirational Chronicle of Poems for the Soul is a labor of my love and a dream come true. For as long as I can remember, I have been writing poems, and the desire to publish them one day was always in my heart. Due to the busyness of life, I was too occupied to focus my attention on doing so, but I always made time to write as I felt led or inspired to do so by God which is how I was able to bring forth this book.

Penned with love from a once-wounded Soldier who has found healing in writing and self-introspection, I invite you to prepare your mind to receive and your heart to heal as you embark on a journey with me as you read *From the Heart of a Warrior: An Inspirational Chronicle of Poems for the Soul.* This book is a labor of love and sacrifice over the years, and each poem depicts a part of my personal life experience and journey, both good and bad.

The question: *what's life without challenges?* is often asked and as a military veteran with more than 26 years of service, I've learned to see beyond the darkness and uncertainty in this thing we call life. As a result, I can access the door that opens to my peace, joy, hope, love, and, most of all, safety, and I encourage you to do the same as you read through each section. Allow yourself to visualize the words as a movie playing in your mind and allow yourself to feel the emotions that accompany each scene, so you can connect with the spiritual and emotional energy of each poem.

Additionally, at the end of each section, there's a reflection area that brings each theme to a close and provides some journal prompts that relate to the theme of that section. I desire that you take a few minutes to read and answer each question, ensuring that you write it down so you can reflect on it and implement the areas that require you to act.

From *The Heart of a Warrior: An Inspirational Chronicle of Poems for the Soul* is unlike any other book of poems because:

+ It will incite joy through melody.

+ It will set you on a path to self-introspection and self-discovery.

+ It will soothe you because poems are therapeutic for both the writer and the reader.

+ It will trigger memories and emotions, promoting empathy's emotional and personal development.

+ It will improve your critical thinking skills by prompting you to think deeper as the meaning isn't always obvious or one-dimensional.

I invite you to get ready to be moved spiritually and emotionally.

Mendez Frith

My Reflection; My Mirror

Created in the image of God
I bore divine qualities of love
Creativity, wisdom, and success
My mirror reflects the man I have become
Showing how much I've grown

My pigmentation reflects my traits and heritage
My face displays my emotions
My eyes glare the truth deep within my soul
Depicting my pain and how much I've been hurt
Expressing my feelings from deep within

My emotions and shame, beneath my guilt,
Have run through my watery eyes
Down my bruised and chiseled body
My journey, past travels and disappointments
Broken dreams, promises, relationships and commitments
All have reflected in the mirror

Often times I feel lonely and insecure
As my past travels try to re-chain me
So, I call on Jesus to be my company
He's carried me so far,
From distant journeys so I won't return
Starving my distractions and feeding my focus

I look at you staring, emulating my every move
Shedding the light on my secrets, strengths and weaknesses
My love and hate, indulgences, compassion and confidence

My reputation, character, pain, joy, happiness and sadness
My image, commitment, passions and consciousness

I attracted that which I expected
Reflected all that I desired
Became the person I respected
While mirroring whom I admired
All while managing expectations
And having ideas and visions

I grew stronger because I was weak
I became fearless because I was afraid
I became a beacon of light, after God's heart
I am wiser because I once was foolish
My image is a reflection in the mirror
Of which I alone can change

Rather than staring in the mirror,
Tell me the things I've never thought or seen
Reveal the true sense of confidence and pride
The reflection I see is unlike the views of others
If only I could see myself from your mirror

"

"Let this be a time where you see yourself less through your own eyes and more through the eyes of the one who created you."
Ashley Hetherington

"

SECTION ONE

Faith

*Therefore, everyone who hears these words of mine
and puts them into practice is like a wise man
who built his house on the rock.*
Mathew 7:24

Faith means having complete trust or confidence in someone or something. Faith is the assurance of things hoped for, the confidence of things not seen. Faith can also mean believing in yourself, which further means having confidence in your abilities. As a result, you can trust yourself to do what you say you'll do and know that those efforts will result in the desired outcomes.

My Identity

Often times defined by one's race or color
Name, nationality or culture
Gender orientation, wealth and seldom religion;
My identity is neither internal nor external
What's your identity?

Why question who I am?
Is it the pigmentation of my skin, my style and fashion?
Or is it the accent with which I speak?
My identity is not dependent on what others think
It's uniquely created by my Lord and Savior Jesus Christ

My identity is a representative of my savior
It rests not upon what I know but who I am in Christ
The things that He has and is now doing in my life
My identity is that of Jesus Christ who provides all of my needs
Allow Christ to define your identity before society defines you

My identity isn't about traits— positive or negative
Strengths and weaknesses, talents and passions
My identity is God's power that determines actions and behaviors
Never explain your identity to others

My identity is the unavoidable part of my life
That shapes my actions
And builds a reputation unlike any other
A vector destined to a future that's greater than all
My identity is that of Christ; unique in His own image

Men judge your identity on their perception of you
But God judges according to one's character
My identity cannot be replicated, bought or sold

My identity is not based on the words of others
My identity and value comes from Christ

My identity is a continuous process
That must be constantly earned
So understand yourself and become better
My identity is endorsed by God
What's yours?

66

"But to all who believed him and accepted him, he gave the right to become children of God."
John 1: 12

99

The Lighthouse

Towering above the ocean's edge, a lighthouse stands
Alone, grounded on the solid foundation of the land
Exposed to the elements, battered by storms and tidal waves
It's a pillar to guide ashore; a mission to save

Rotating endlessly in the dark, towering over every wave
Brilliantly dazzling across the calm or stormy seas
Like a guardian angel, it illuminates a beacon of hope
Extending a guidance and hand of comfort

Our heavenly father is our lighthouse
He guides us through our battles and storms
Through the midnight slumber and raging seas
GOD is the light of the world

"

"Thy word is a lamp unto my feet,
and a light unto my path."
Psalm 119:105

"

The Price Of The Cross

Our loving creator and Supreme Being
The all-powerful, all-knowing spirit composed being
Sacrificed for political expediency
He became a victim of injustices
The punishment of my sins rest upon Him
CHRIST, the spotless Lamb became our savior

Innocent, perfect without sin or blemish
Alone, in deep sorrow, JESUS frequently knelt and prayed
Soaked and burdened with the torrential downpour of our sins
Overwhelmed by spiritual suffering, pain and agony
His soul deeply grieved to the point of death

Abandoned and betrayed by those within his inner circle,
He endured the rejection of those who closely knew him
Arrested, blasphemed, judged, mocked and abused
Slandered on false charges brought against him
JESUS became the emblem of suffering and shame

Compelled to bear his burdened cross, wearing a crown of thorns
JESUS struggled through the streets of Jerusalem
All the way to Calvary – Golgotha "Place of a Skull"
His sweat like droplets of blood, fell upon the ground
In anguish His life slowly drifted away

Anticipating the scourging and sorrowful hours on the cross
Insulted, taunted, spat upon, tortured and terrorized
Blind folded, humiliated, brutally flogged and whaled
Inflicting excruciating pain, His skin frayed as blood splattered
CHRIST suffered beyond the deepest agony or physical pain

Forsaken, separated from God
A broken fellowship, severed relationship from God
His Hopeless despair and blackness of depravity
CHRIST avenged our sins with His body as a ransom on the Cross
CHRIST demonstrated his love so we may live in righteousness

Our sinful ways were crucified with CHRIST
That sin and temptation may lose its power
For our eternal life and a commitment to GOD
With countless thoughts, actions, kindness and blessings
To live and love everlasting, never to forsake thee

Nothing that you and I have done is beyond God's forgiveness
The just for the un-just, the righteous for the un-righteous
JESUS CHRIST the servant paid a debt he did not owe
Greater than the screaming nerves, agony and pain

Condemned, nailed high, spread wide
JESUS was wounded for my transgressions
JESUS was bruised for my iniquities
Beaten and broken beyond recognition

The price of the Cross was not mere silver or gold
But the atoning sacrifice paid by CHRIST
By His scars I am healed; JESUS paid it all.
We owe a debt we can't repay

"But he was wounded for our transgressions, he was bruised for our iniquities; the chastisement of our peace was upon him, and by his stripes we are healed."
Isaiah 53:5

Reflections

Below are five reflective questions to ask yourself about your faith to begin to stand firm in your spiritual or personal truth. The point of these self-reflective questions is to encourage you to look inwardly and make sure your foundation is built on unshakable faith.

1. **Does pride interfere with faith?**

2. **Are you ready to give a defense for your faith?**

3. **What areas of faith do you struggle with?**

4. **Do you have any doubts about your faith?**

5. **Are you prepared to tackle anything that contradicts with your faith?**

SECTION TWO

Family

"Family is where life begins and love never ends."

Growing up as a young child, I was raised in a family who were united and guided by certain beliefs and morals. My family ensured that my needs took preference above their own and love was not limited to circumstances or time. The world as we know it is a very busy place, everyone young and old has so many commitments which can make it difficult for families to spend time together. However, all relationships need attention most importantly families. As I penned these poems that you are about to read, I was inspired by my family; the ones who cradled and protected me from a young child into adulthood and the one I created on my own. May you connect with memories of your family as you ponder upon the poems below.

Lessons from Papa

Not so long ago, when I was a boy,
I drove you crazy as if you were a toy
With all my *yes's* and *no's*
Why not?'s and *want to's,* were such a joy
Yet you never ran out of things to say
You held no grudges, you had no fears

For all the years of living in and sharing your world,
There remain stories untold
You taught me to do what's right
You taught me how to do things right
You taught me how to survive and build a fire
You gave me much hope and desire

From a boy, you gladly raised and tutored me
With patience, you were a teacher
Bits of life's wisdom you openly share
To work hard, play hard and do my best
You prepared me for life and its opportunities
Though you didn't answer all, you listened to my every question

Without me realizing
Education was the key instrument of my day
Therefore, you showed me the way
To school, work, play and pray
My moral compass of fair play
You instilled discipline, honesty and respect
You oversaw the things I did and speak

My happiest memories remain in my heart
As I accepted the challenges, I believed and achieved
Your generosity touched the lives of many

You weren't rich, but we always had enough
Your shoulders beared the weight of your family
While your peace and happiness influenced a community

You loved and cared for all you knew
Friends and family; and those who knew you
Through your sons and daughters your love is reflected
Through generations your voice is echoed
On their faces your smiles are reflected
Steadfast and glowing for all to see

A heart of pure compassion; submerged in love
By the hands of the Almighty sitting above
You molded me to become a man
So, I journeyed my path and became a Soldier
Overcame the challenges; exhaled and propelled
And soared victoriously

As I reflect on memories of the years' past,
I envision you sitting on the veranda
With friends and family conversing and smiling
Slamming dominoes, handing out six-loves
While sipping a glass of your favorite Brandy
Never wearing a frown

66

"He was a man of courage and strength. He never spoke much so you may never know his thoughts."
Mendez Frith

99

Mother, I Thank You

M: MAGNIFICIENT
O: OUTSTANDING
T: TENDER
H: HONORABLE
E: EXTRAORDINARY
R: REMARKABLE

Mother, you are my voice of reason
You gave me life; you dressed and taught me
You shouted at me; you fought for me
During my times of trouble, you showed no fear
No trace of insecurities but a better cure
My mother's love is a home and place of shelter

Mother, you raised and taught me
Like a mold you shaped then groomed me
With your mighty hands, you protected me
With your tender touch, you disciplined me
With your words you gave a voice to me
By your actions, you paved the way for me
With patience, you loved and cared for me

You journeyed; my joy, burdens and pains you bear
You marched; away you wiped my tears
Quietly, you calmed my fears
My disappointments you soothed
In me you instilled and inspired confidence

In the shadows you stood proud and strong
Through your toil, blood, sweat and tears
You made sacrifices as I grew into my own

You're the mother I didn't appreciate until I was grown
Now you're the one whom I'm proud to call my own

You've always understood the things I say and do
Overlooked my faults and brought out the best in what I do
In my moments of failures and brokenness
You picked me up when I fell to weaknesses
Together we celebrate success and achievements

You're the driving force that shaped my choices
With your love and courage, you inspire me every day
You spread joy and happiness in your own special way
With a tender smile that guides my way
You're the sunshine that lightens my day

For your love and joy, sacrifices and struggles, I thank you
For your courage, faith and fierceness, I thank you
For your tears, strength and wisdom, I thank you
For your prayers and fasting, I thank you
For your gift of yourself you've given, I thank you
For your time and patience, I thank you

Thank you will never be enough for all that you have done
For allowing me to grow into my own
For being my counselor and my guardian angel
For letting me learn and wanting nothing in return
None of me and more of you is what you gave

But most importantly,
My hand you held for a while and my heart forever
Thank you for being my Mom

"

"You may have stumbled, and sometimes you may have fallen. And just like the sun that always rise, you rise before the break of dawn."
Mendez Frith

"

My Father

F: Faithful
A: Anchor
T: Teacher
H: Hero
E: Ever loving
R: Rock

A man of action and of few words
Sometimes I wondered if we lived in two different worlds
My father didn't tell me how to live
By his actions, he allowed me to watch him live

My father learned and lived by principles
He believes in being prompt
If he's not 15 minutes early then he is late
He is rough, tough, honest, and polite

My father is one of the most unsung, unpraised heroes
He shoulders the weight of the world for his household
Known as one of the most valuable assets in our family
A man of unmatched strength and integrity

He's our guide, our protector, and teacher
He scolded us when we broke the rules
He believed in us even when we failed
He shines with pride when we succeed

He's a prayer warrior and a man of faith
He is a good man living in a society that devalues men
He's admired and loved by many
He's a hero and friend within our community

The rock and cornerstone
Brick by brick, he held his own
Building the city with his hands
To change the skyline of the land

"

"What makes you a man isn't the ability to have a child – it's the courage to raise one."
Barack Obama

"

Rescue

Life is filled with initial greetings and final passing's
Where many enter our lives for a purpose or reason
Some journey for the sunshine and rain; whatever the season
Some for a lifetime of pleasures, laughter, tear-drops and pain
But only one for a century

As we celebrate the life of PAPPA
An honest man and friend of many
A friend of age and guide for our youth
With a virtuous heart and a friend of the truth
Very few with such knowledge and wisdom informed

From the depths of his deepest valleys
To the midst of his hardest fights
In rising flames and pouring rain
His hard-working hands are laid to rest
His weight bearing feet are laid weightless
In peace, free from the realities of life
GOD has rescued him

He lived in the moment; with lots to see, he took the scenic route of life
With a lamp unto his feet and a light unto his path
The guided steps of the LORD he followed
No task whether simple, small, or great left undertaken
With a willing heart and obedient hands
He mustered the strength and courage
For us he did them all

He was a man of courage and strength
He never spoke much so you would never know his thoughts
His life was a blessing
His legacy is a guide, recorded in history

His memories remain our treasure
He was loved beyond oceans and borders
He will be missed beyond measures

A giant in our lifetime.
Spanned 5 scores plus 4
A man of high integrity and character
A farmer, a carpenter and father who poured out for years
He raised tradesmen, chefs, ministers and caregivers
Healthcare professionals, civil servants and educators
Engineers, musicians, Soldiers and law enforcers

The rock, anchor and foundation
The head but not the stone
Life was just his stepping stone on his journey home
But from his duties as head of his home
From his ups and downs, his highs and gut-wrenching lows
Under the weight of high expectations
God came to rescue him home

With a wealth of experience and survival
He endured affliction and tribulation
A fighter who fought with ferocity
Decorated with scars and surrounded by stars
We dare not wish him back

It breaks our hearts to see him go
On that night GOD called him home
For the rest of our lives, he will be greatly missed
From deep within our souls, hidden tears will flow
Expressing messages of unspeakable love
So, don't await the grief to pass you by; but dance and celebrate
And with your heads held high, miss him for a while

PAPPA lived a wonderful life
Leaving so many wonderful memories
And just like the change of the seasons
We're witnessing the changing of the guard
A transfer from generation to generation
His voyage has ended; His spirit ascended
Claiming his eternal reward from our heavenly creator

His body was weary and broken
Calmly under his breath he whispered
Saying, "RESCUE ME! I have nothing left."
And GOD heard his voice

GOD answered the call of his failing voice
His soul was released; set free by the SON
In peace, he laid his burdens down
Gentle holding unto the outstretched hand of GOD
And quietly he left us all

"

"*You molded me to become a man, so I journeyed my path and became a Soldier. Overcame the challenges; exhaled, propelled and sored victoriously.*"
Mendez Frith

"

Unity in the Community

From the earth we are all made
Equally created by our heavenly Father
To each other we are not equal
Yet each other we don't know
As a people, we all must do better
And uphold the human rights of each other

Emancipated youths from destitute Communities
For decades their lives have been targeted; some ended in tragedies
For decades we all reside in fear
For decades too many tears we share
For decades too many suffering
Decade after decade, seemingly no one cares

Police officers have become gun willing
Badge wearing, street beat cops stand above the law
Protected perpetrators of crimes on those vulnerable
Applying systematic pressure; playing mindful games
Afflicting pain and anguish
While exempt from accountability and punishment

A socialist war against democracy
Our youth must learn critical thinking and individuality
Like mindless drones our youth's roam the streets destroying society
We must examine our policies and procedures
Identify the nature and extent of our problems
In order to relieve the tensions and perceptions

Assassinations and unspeakable acts of barbarism
Juveniles in the streets victimized
Pawned in a system of racial and physical violence
With shattered hopes, dreams, promises and future

Left with empty space in their lives that needs fulfilling
To become survivors, the fight we have to be willing

A system designed to cheat people
A system designed to delete people
How much more suffering; how much more pain?
Seen our youth's grow; their lives prematurely taken
Lay down your guns; cease the violence across our communities
Police officers and citizens; let's unite as one across our communities

Americans, parents, blacks, whites and hispanics
Community leaders, pastors, teachers, politicians stand in unity
Mother's, father's, husband's and wives' stand forth
Sons, daughter's, brother's and sister's your lives have worth
Unite together in peaceful protests and marches
Unite together in campaigns; be advocates for a cause
Let's congregate together across our communities

Communicate, stimulate discussions and develop solutions
Reaching active consensus, build relationships
Be accountable, respect, build trust and expand freedom
Let's play, work and live in unity
Across our community, let's build a spirit of humanity

Let's all emulate a better lifestyle
Parents teach your children how to live right
Police officers risk their lives daily
Police officers serve and protect our communities daily
Police officers deserve our gratitude and respect daily
Our communities and police departments must forge a close bond

Unity in the community must be a dedicated and fulfilled promise
Unity in our community is not a cause based on injustice
Unity in our community is the act of a courageous few
Working side by side, protecting the rights of humanity
Unity in our community is a fulfilled promise by police officers and citizen's
Working side by side, protecting our communities

"

"Finally, all of you have unity of mind, sympathy, brotherly love, a tender heart, and a humble mind."
1 Peter 3:8

"

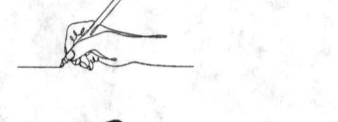

We Celebrate You

You're a daughter, a sister, an aunt, a God-mother and a mother
A prayer warrior and a courageous fighter
A pathfinder and trail blazer
You mastered the combination of strength and power
For all your accolades, we celebrate you

Created and defined by no man, you're writing your own legacy
By reversing history and telling your own story
You are essential to the life of your family and communities
You remain faithful, and many a devoted pillar of your church

God fearing, hardworking, and well respected
You cheered, you shared, you gave and you prayed
Through selflessness, you invested emotionally, and spiritually
Through sacrifices you poured into us physically and financially

You are women of immeasurable value
You are disciples with a ministry
You bring your gifts of love, blessings, kindness, and affirmation
Full of wisdom, you live according to God's word

You are all women with grace, mercy, energy and beauty
Clothed with strength, dressed and deeply rooted with integrity
More precious than any jewels or rubies
You all have a heart made of gold

With a network of support, strength and character
You've towered over your circumstances
You are the broken pieces of pottery
Beautifully placed back together

You are women of strength, independence and intelligence
Beyond measure, you are loved and valued

You are not a second choice; to you there is no equal
To no other you can be compared

For your passion and compassion, you thrive
You're the driving force that shapes a generation
You may have stumbled, and sometimes you may have fallen
And just like the sun you rise before the break of dawn
With your love and courage, you inspire us all

You are royal, you are queens
For all of your grooming and contributions to our lives
We empower, elevate and celebrate you
Not only for this month but for your lifetime

66

"The empowered woman is powerful beyond measure and beautiful beyond description."
Steve Maraboli

99

Reflections

Below are a few reflective questions to ask yourself about your relationship with your family.

The point of these questions is to encourage you to look inwardly to ensure you have a solid foundation and support.

1. Who was the most influential person in your family?

2. What are some life lessons you were taught that played a significant role in your upbringing even to today?

3. Write a fictional perfect day with your family– the best one you can imagine.

4. What does the meaning of the word "family" mean to you?

5. Is family more about blood relations or chosen loved ones for you?

SECTION THREE

Healing

"Healing may not be so much about getting better, as about letting go of everything that isn't you – all of the expectations, all of the beliefs – and becoming who you are."
Rachel Naomi Remen

When I think about healing, I immediately think about wanting to return to myself again— without the pain or the memory of what makes me feel unwell. There's a deep need and desire to be in our natural state of well-being, where we are one with our mind, body, and soul. As I was going through my healing journey, these poems were a part of my healing process, which aided in me restoring the balance in my body, mind, and soul. I invite you to read these poems with an open mind to experience healing. Everyone will need emotional healing at some point, as we all experience challenges and complex emotions that need processing.

A Place to Speak

A place to speak
A safe place in the intimate company of a friend
Where an open heart lingers and share burdens
Share in true communion with one another
A place to pursue and build authentic relationships

To a friend, you come with your hunger
So, whom is that friend that you should seek their hours to kill?
Always seek your friend with hours to live
For it is his to fill your need about your emptiness
So, let's linger with open hearts

A place to speak
A place to express and communicate among a friend
A place where true friends gather in search of peace
To share their burdens, and secrets, dreams and stories
Where desires, expectations, thoughts are born and shared

"

"When your friend speaks his mind, you fear not the "nay" in your own mind, nor do you withhold the "ay."
Kahlil Gibran

"

Be the Moon

Beautifully out of place during times of daylight
Perfectly placed among the galaxies at night
To the moon, the sun sets and yields its way
Without stealing the night away
One fades as the other rises
The moon belongs to the night

She prefers the brilliant company among the galaxies
Perfectly placed and sought among the stars
A teacher of gradualness and deliberation
Like the universe with such perfect details
She slowly gives birth to oneself
Completes a perfect work like the universe

Secluded in heaven's eyes
Illuminating our path from the glorious skies
The good and bad, the ugly and the beautiful
The right and wrong of the dark the moon unveils
Revealing the fullest that surrounds us
The moon knows all our nighttime secrets

Under the illumination of the moon,
Seeds the conception of beautiful thoughts
The nurturing of ideas and dreams
The development of assumptions
That gives your lungs a reason to breathe

The moon is the birth canal of visions
And you are just like the moon
Encircled by a cast of brilliant stars
Beautiful, yet full of imperfections
Through the griefs, the storms, the wind and rain

Through light and darkness, aches and pains
The moon remained resilient

No matter how many times you fall, keep rising
Dance to the rhythm through the seasons
Be the moon that illuminates in the darkest hour
Be the moon that brightens someone's darkest hour
No need for a comparison between you and other's
Release the brightest light of your soul; shine when it's your time

66

"The sun loves the moon so much that he dies every night to let her breathe and in return, she reflects his love."
Jeffrey Fry

99

Emotional Baggage

We make mistakes and learn; we fall and rise
We carry expressions of smiles, but inside we're crying
Inside I'm trying but it feels like I'm dying
Unpleasant memories feel like a torture
And circumstances attempt to alter my future
So hard to let things go

Who am I to judge while I walk imperfect?
Caught up in the cycle and pages of our lives
Trapped in a defensive and protective state
Paralyzed by the burdens and sorrows
Fallen victim to the circumstances I encounter
As emotional baggage piles with a hefty and stifling price

Imprisoned by the experiences and clutters of yesterday
Denial, disappointments, deception, depression
The lies, resentment, regrets and desperation
Guilt, low self-esteem, weaknesses and shortfalls
A daunting desire to re-visit the past
Baggage comes with a price that seems to last

The scars you can't erase; the truth you can't replace
Open wounds, hurt, pain, bitterness and betrayal
Fears, anger, envy, greed, lust and jealousy
Secrets, pride, addictions and obsessions
Missed opportunities, broken dreams and promises
Emotional baggage inhabits a wounded soul

Troubled yet not distressed; perplexed but not in despair
Prosecuted but not forsaken; cast down but not destroyed
You may encounter difficulties but never be defeated
Let go of the unforgiving past and bypass the storms

Exhale the painful memories and climb the mountains
Your circumstances must never determine who you become

Identify and define; erase the waste that claimed your past
Face your fears, sorrows and emotions with courage
Conquer your fears of the past; step into the future
Break the chains of emotional baggage
Forgive others and seek forgiveness
Make a commitment to live better

We all can rise and overcome
Love yourself, accept your faults and mistakes
Build positive and meaningful relationships
Grow, evolve and embrace your opportunities
Transform into a paradigm with new beginnings
Where freedom patiently awaits your claim

66

"It's time to create an unbreakable love for yourself that cannot be broken by the unkind words and actions of others."
Tiffany Moule

99

I Was Busy!

Broken by conflicts, wounded by wars
I was busy fighting, defeating and deleting my adversary
Navigating the indiscernible scenes and tragedies of war
Busy trying to avoid the attention, sorrows and anger
Suppressing my pain, hurt and covering my scars

I was busy heading to the sites of destruction and chaos
I was busy rejecting the impacts and inflicted memories
Avoiding the feeling of guilt for my wounded comrades
Often times, questioning my reasons for fighting
I was busy not protecting my body, mind and soul

I was busy sacrificing my time, energy and resources
Avoiding memories of firefights and nightmares
Running with shattered dreams and years of invisible tears
Despite my achievements, badges, medals and awards
In the end, I realized that not many really cared

I was busy running the streets that exposed me to the night lights
Running from the dark days that kept me awake at nights
The negative thoughts, unclean images that flowed through my mind
I was busy running and leaving my weaknesses, and failures behind
I was busy avoiding repentance, running from my sins, and convictions

I was busy suffering in silence with thoughts flowing through my mind
I was busy, attempting to overcome my extreme rages—one of a kind
Isolated, numb, subduing my irregular feelings and emotions
Not asking for help, I was busy solving my problems with no one listening
On a one-way glide, it was just me myself and I descending

I was busy reminiscing and running from my destructive past
And all the negative memories I wish I could erase

All the tricks and worldly habits I acquired along the way
Realizing I can't move forward while tracing my last
Busy while not giving up hope of a better tomorrow

I was busy, seeking growth, opportunities, and making changes
Dismissing my doubters, carving paths and shattering ceilings
Becoming someone like many thought I would
While so many others were intimidated by my potential

I was unclear when I repeatedly said I was O.K
I was busy in a way most people may never understand
I was busy in search of healing
I was busy praying for GOD's outstretched hand
And I refuse to apologize to anyone for being BUSY

"

"I was dishonest when I said I was O.K, and I refuse to apologize to anyone for being BUSY."
Mendez Frith

"

I Was Running

Boom, boom, the sound of lightning and thunder
Incoming artillery landed and exploded all around
I dawned my kit, grabbed my radio and weapon
I started running

Stuck in the middle of an artillery strike
I found myself running from the disaster, chaos, sorrows and fight
Navigating the indiscernible scenes and tragedies of war
Suppressing my pain, hurt and covering my scars

The further away I got, the closer they landed
Through the hills and valleys, I ran
Over land and bridges, I ran
Boom, boom, they kept on exploding

Boom, boom, shrapnel metal flying
My blood's rushing, heart's pumping
Vision's blurry as I'm drenched in sweat
My nerve's frayed as I'm consumed with fear

Out of the dark I was running to save my life
I had no reason for looking back
I can't move forward while looking back
Out of my midnight sleep, I jumped
This is another nightmare

66

"Let us run with endurance the race that is set before us."
Hebrews 12:1 ESV

99

The Sun

The marvelous and luminous celestial body
Whose fierce spirit wonders the universe?
The source of energy and light
The sustainer of universal life
Who radiates and illuminates the planets

Wild, free and untamed
The juggler and ruler of the day
That shines in space and time
Across distant places and dimensions

She elevates far beyond the clouds
She eliminates the darkness
And scorches the shade-less desert
Embracing her mighty powers

The center of the revolving solar system
Her light remains brightly shining
Her spirit within burns forever
To the places where darkness cannot roam

From east to west, the sun glows
With extended and nurturing rays
Streaming energy across the universe
Shining brighter than all other cast of stars
This is how I see who others are

At sunset, she kneels beyond the horizon
Where her beauty last only a few
Yielding to the moon as she rises
As one rises the other fades
No matter how many times she kneels she rises

Her rays connect deep inside my soul
Her light and spirit guide my way
I've seen, and felt her beauty
I've known no other warmth like hers

Despite the rain and storms
Despite the clouds and shadows
I relish in her presence; Peace be still
The wind and waves bow to her will

Known throughout the universe
As a star that projects power
A legend, a legacy and diary that never close
She writes all my secrets
Across the beautiful parchment sky

Too good to not believe
You give life, you restore
You give hope, you reveal
The beauty to what I don't understand

Be my light; be my guide, my way, be my will
From up above your love, you shine
Down on me for the world to see
Shining your light on me

"

"I believe in Christ, like I believe in the sun –
not because I can see it, but by
it I can see everything else."
C.S. Lewis

"

True Friends

With many I have interacted, but chosen are only a few
In the midst of hard times and conflicts, our friendship grew
Like great men we formed and survived as a tightly knitted crew
While many acquaintances rolled away just like the morning dew

Real friends are the one's whom you can depend
A person who will listen and not condemn
Friends increases your value, fight for you, and support you
Friends also need you, include you, respect and encourage you

A friend is priceless, a friend is a treasure
The one who knows your weaknesses but highlights your strength
They're like the angels who meet you at the point of your need
And the stars you often don't see but they know exactly where you are

When everyone has failed you
After all the fusses and fighting, the wins and losses,
True friends will never do you wrong or steer you wrong
True friends will never change but will always come along
True friends are dependable and will hold you accountable

I no longer foster or harvest meaningless relationships
I no longer force interactions or unnecessary conversations
As acquaintances decrease in numbers, you realize who matters
Who never did, who won't and who always will

True friends reside in our hearts
True friends will never part or tear you apart
Despite different points of view or disagreements
Friends build a relationship that will forever last

"Rare as is true love, true friendship is rarer."
Jean de la Fontaine

We Talked

We sat, and we talked on a bench underneath the old shack
Releasing the anger and toxic feeling of a horrific attack
Our profession has our Soldiers catching up to God quicker
As no one else understood the devastating occurrence

We've been drawn together not just by our color, culture and nationality
But by our profession, a calling, service, morals, and duty
We've both walked similar paths in the sand
And climbed the mountains clinging to the almighty hand

We're both in a mindset of darkness,
Waiting for the break of day to see the light
With similar endeavors and endings
We talked, we confided to gain strength

Words may have fell short in times of crisis
In a fight that brought us to our knees
It felt like we could hardly breathe
To tell our heart to beat again

A friend is the most valuable gift you'll ever need
Someone to talk or listen
To escape the darkness into the light

"

"Healing takes courage, and we all have courage, even if we have to dig a little to find it."
Tori Amos

"

Reflection

Having to face our problems and struggle every now and then is inevitable. No matter how much we believe we have planned for setbacks, challenges will come unexpectedly and cause pain. Navigating through these uncomfortable emotions is never a walk in the park. Still, no matter how difficult, you can overcome every obstacle through perseverance and resilience. To help with recovery and healing, here's a few reflective journal prompts to help you do some self-introspection regarding your healing journey.

1. What would you want to be known for?

2. In what ways have you healed already?

3. What makes you feel sad and depressed?

4. What are the things you feel grateful for in life?

5. What, in your perspective, are your best attributes?

6. If you could rewrite an experience from your past, what would it be?

7. When do you feel calm, peaceful, and in touch with your inner self?

SECTION FOUR

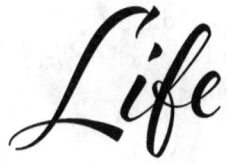

"The time is always right to do what is right."
— *Martin Luther King Jr.*

Life is a concept that can only be lived in the present moment. It is the aspect of existence. Every day, one should strive to be better at something. Nothing can be done yesterday or tomorrow. Life presents us with opportunities and challenges. It is often important to take a moment and reflect on yourself. I hope you enjoy the poems up ahead.

A Beach Without Water

The desert, a dry and thirsty land
A landscape comprised of barren surfaces
Rocky plains and ridges of sand dunes
Where there's no trace, sound or smell of water
A land that offers no forgiveness

A sparseness of vegetation
With minimum soil development
Of which few lonely leafless trees scattered
Shrubbery quailed, survived by roots grown deep
Under extreme heat, not a shelter of shade to spare

Extreme temperatures with minimum precipitation
A place with limited nature in its existence
Very few tribes and nomads
An environment with the feel of a life sentence
Only the strong survive

A sandy forest without a shore
Where there's no shadow under the sun
But sprawling winds and sweltering temperatures
Prevailing winds blowing hot and dry
That raises dust, producing sand storms

Welcome to the open desert
Where civilization ends
And reality begins

"

"*The beach is not always a place.
Sometimes it's a feeling.*"
Unknown Author

"

Beautiful Places; Smiling Faces

Beautiful places, smiling faces
From the warmth and sincerity of the people
The vibes, local cuisine and culture
Tropical climate, beaches, and nature
Lavish all-inclusive vacation resorts
All are welcome with eager and open arms

From the clear, sunny and blue skies
Private cottages and suites along the garden paths
To the resorts where the pool meets the beaches
Dramatic seaside cliffs overlooking the ocean
Where the wind blows and the seas come washing ashore
Inspiration that paints the perfect picture

From the Blue Mountains and hidden lagoons
To the Reggae, Mayfield, Reach, and YS Falls
Where streams of water flows through the ravines
To the hazy Blue Hole mineral springs
And the Doctor's Cave beach in Montego Bay
Where nature charms you with its beauty

Explore the gorgeous and tropical landscapes
Climb the majestic Dunn's River Falls
Suspend from the zip-lines above
Descend through tropical jungle
Dive from the cliffs; swim and snorkel the under waters
A must-see for one and all to adventure

Acres of marijuana growing on the Blue Mountains
Pure and natural beauty; it's of the highest grade
No cross pollination, it's the natural breed
Prettiest of flowers; scented above all roses
Proclaimed celebrity among all trees
Known as the healer of the nation

View the magnificent sunrise from the east
Glowing through the mist and scattering clouds
Rainbow colors reflects the sunset in the west
Slowly descending below the horizon
Experience the beauty of the moonrise
As the beautiful cities comes to life at nightfall

Tropical fruits, vegetables and exotic spices
An abundance of freshly caught seafood
The zesty jerk pork and chicken dishes
Ackee and salt-fish, rice and peas
Curried goat, ox-tail, Manish-water
All from the base of the Jamaican cuisine

Smile; enjoy the synthesis and friendliness of the local Jamaicans
The soul and spirit of the island lies within the people
The people's culture and beauty radiate across the island
Indulge in the consumption of the tropical beverages
Groove to the musical rhythms and beats of the sweet reggae music
Where there's always beautiful places and smiling faces

Out of Many; One People. Jamaica

"

"The best thing to hold onto in life is each other."
Audrey Hepburn

"

Born With Sight but Lack Vision

Sight is the function of the eyes
The faculty or power of seeing
One's ability to observe or catch a glimpse
Sight is the perception of objects seen through one's eyes

Sight allows one to see problems and struggles
Sight; the power to look without seeing

Vision; a mental perception or regard
A preferred picture of what's to be achieved
Something inspirational, worth chasing
A vision provides guidance and focus

Sight without vision blinds hopes, dreams and future
Sight without vision cripples one's soul
As humans, we have sight to see but lack depth
As humans we're born with sight; but we lack vision

Without vision we lack conviction
To encourage and influence outcomes
Without vision we become slaves to our society
Doing far less than what God intended

Vision; the driving force behind progress
That ignites one's passion and commitment
To find, develop and resolve solutions
That transforms dreams of reality into greatness

Man's greatest gift is a vision
Your vision is interpreted through your life's events
Your vision has neither borders nor limitations
Live your life through vision, beyond sight

Your sight leads and guides you
Your vision transforms you
Be not conformed by your sight
Be transformed by your mind and vision

Without vision God's people will perish
Without vision God's nations will perish
With vision we can change the world
Transform your sight into God's vision

"

"Where there is no vision, the people perish."
Proverbs 29:18

"

Life

Life; the human aspect of existence; presents itself only once
A cycle that cannot be duplicated, paused or restarted
With no warrantees, extensions, guarantees or second chances
Filled with dreams, aspirations, challenges and broken promises
Life only provides possibilities and opportunities

A combination of roots, cultures and worldly flavors
Relationships, requirements and expectations
The bitterness, gloominess, sadness, doubts and failures
Human imperfections and powers; systems of checks and balances
Life brings us more than our fair share of triumphs and blessings

Life is an adventure, compiled with detours and derailments
Accidents and pitfalls, sorrows, crosses and trials
Where mistakes are teachers and weakness become a strength
Where turmoil' and sadness turns to happiness
And energy is a gift proliferated into good

Life is shortly lived with each breath, moments and seconds
Between thoughts, space, distance and time
It's a vision for the wise; a game to the fool
So capture the great moments; focus on what's important
Value your memories; learn from your mistakes

We are created to succeed; destined to be victors
Equipped to overcome; anointed and appointed to prosper
Face your trials and discover your strengths
Don't await the storms to pass but dance through the rain
Climb the mountains and sail the waves to overcome

With ongoing difficulties and daily struggles to fight
Tragedies to face and setbacks to overcome

A duty to perform and a journey to complete
Where your decisions define your direction
Your direction will determine your destination

A puzzle to solve, a mystery to unfold
Life is beautiful with an abundance of happiness
Filled with preciousness that requires protection
Where joy and sadness are expressed through tears
As we dream, believe and achieve

A life with struggle results in a life of success
The past we cannot change; yet the future we can influence
Be the star that illuminates the dark
Inhale the challenges; exhale and propel visions
And soar victoriously

Life is a mixture of sunshine and rain
Relentless struggles, and events
Pleasures, laughter, tear-drops and pain
Life is a beautiful experience to live and love
Do more than exist. Live with a purpose!

66

*"You only have one life to live.
Make sure it's yours."*
Eleanor Brown

99

Giving Thanks All Year 'Round

As the summer season slowly drifts away,
Autumn season slowly approaches
With windy skies and decreasing temperatures
The temperate deciduous forest cycles
Green leaves of the trees turn tan and brown
Then slowly they all fall to the ground
The feel of thanksgiving fills the air

Shades of dark red, purple plum, brown and tangerine
With golden harvest themed décor fills the halls
Many paintings of the past hang on the walls
Coupled with an excitement of baked aromas
While friends and loved ones gather together
To dine and dwell in the hearts of each other

Platters of specially prepared meals,
Fancy plates, dinnerware, and folks well dressed
As we hold hands, taking time, to give thanks
Mouthwatering, taste buds quivering
As family and friends dine in joy
Experiencing the moments, saving the memories

Fruits, string beans and salad dressed just right
Baked turkey, lamb chops, ham, stuffing and gravy
Dinner rolls, corn bread, appetizers and corn
Candied sweet potatoes, baked and mashed potatoes

Thanksgiving isn't all about the feast
Thanksgiving is all about gratitude

An opportunity to see the good in our lives
The special friends and family we love
Coupled with blessings both great and small

Let's make thanksgiving our daily living
Let's celebrate thanksgiving through the entire year
Let's be thankful for all the blessings God provides
Let's raise our voices and give God the praises
Let's make every day our Thanksgiving Day
Happy thanksgiving

66

"And whatever you do, in word or deed, or
everything in the name of the lord Jesus,
giving thanks to God the father through him."
Colossians 3:17

99

The Past

Often distracted by yesterday's failures and regrets
Let go and realize that the past is far gone
Allow me to release the past by seizing in the moment
Enjoy the moment. It's filled with joy and happiness
'Cause yesterday will be analyzed tomorrow

We store the past in our mind
The future we clench with our fingers
Contrasting what's gone with the present
And like a weapon we use it against each other

The past we cannot change
We make excuses that we cannot re-write
All we can do is accept it and do better
Forget the past but learn from the experience

The future is where you apply the lesson
Release the unchangeable past
It's a point of reference
Embrace your future head on

"

"You can't go back and change the beginning,
but you can start where you are
and change the ending."
C.S. Lewis

"

The Power of the Tongue

The boaster of things, large and great
The smallest but largest troublemaker
A rebel that stirs up anger
A restless evil, full of deadly poison
A deceitful tongue crushes the human spirit

A fire that chars' relationships
A flame that tarnishes reputations
Defiles the body and sets ablaze the soul
The tongue; a reference to the spoken word
Speaks like a piercing sword
And reveals the messages from the heart

An offensive and defensive weapon
That serves a role of critical importance
Chambered inside the breeched cannon
Like a rocket, it sets to launch
From which words of anger have never won

A wholesome tongue is a tree of life
It humbles its critics, and marvels others
It blesses and ministers Grace unto its hearers
It encourages the broken hearted
It commends, mends and heals relationships

From the tongue comes grand speeches, lectures and praises
With the tongue we sing, pray, preach, bless and prophesy
We exaggerate, curse, scorn, mock, gossip and lie
At the mercy of the tongue, we're subject to die
With the tongue, we ask the question: why?

For moments of carnal lust and intimate pleasure
To conversations of leisure,
Filled with desires, affection and seduction
Attention, excitement and appreciation,
The tongue paints the perfect picture

The truthful tongue speaks and shew forth righteousness
A lying tongue poureth foolishness
The tongue of the wise is health that turns away wrath
False lips speak grievous words and stirs anger
The tongue expresses wisdom and knowledge aright

Wars have been fought because of the tongue
Men have worked themselves into the ground for their tongue
Gone down on their knees begging to keep their tongue
Taken blame, suffered persecution for their tongue
Endured torture and pain because of their tongue

The tongue can no man tame
It harms, corrupts and lay blame
It made men rich and women famous
It has started and ended wars
It changed the course of nations
The tongue holds the power of life and death

"

"Death and life are in the power of the tongue, and those who love it will eat its fruits."
Proverbs 18:21

"

The Present

Life occurs only in the present
The existing moment is the most beautiful,
Unlike the reviews of yesterday's past
So, align your consciousness with the now
And accept the present moment
It is all you'll ever know

Today is the tomorrow you dreamed of yesterday
The opening doors and new opportunities
So, live in the moment and plan your tomorrow
Which brings its own mysteries and unknowns
Joy, peace and blessings

Never allow the blues and sorrows of yesterday
To ruin today's joy, peace, blessings and happiness
So, be occupied by the opportunities of the present
Because if the present moment is neglected,
It will never return

Nothing gets accomplished yesterday or tomorrow
But only in the present-day
Let go of what was, and embrace what is
Seize the moment; launch yourself on every wave
And believe in what is yet to come

Lean not on your own understanding
Don't worry about the unknowns of tomorrow
'Cause to no one the future is secure
Yesterday is history, tomorrow is a mystery
Look closely at what you are constructing
It should be the future you are dreaming!

66

"If you must look back, do so forgivingly. If you must look forward, do love prayerfully. However, the wisest thing you can do is be present in the present...Gratefully."
Maya Angelou

99

The Simple Things in Life

One smile, a simple smile
The symbol of love
Affection, care, comfort
Compassion, sympathy, desire
The smile that makes one's day

The modest details
The minute actions
The simple gestures
Every good deed
The thought of giving hope

Embrace your bestowed gift
Bring happiness to a gloomy world
Make a change the world needs
Encourage kindness, remove negativity
Be optimistic; inspire others

Step beyond the transient boundaries
Let go of thy raging egos
Show off your inner beauty
Spread your token of love
A simple smile

66

"To succeed in life, you need three things: a wishbone, a backbone and a funny bone."
Reba McEntire

99

Time!

There are times, I sit back and relax, thinking…
The beautiful streams, rivers, lakes, falls and oceans I see
The amazing hills, valleys, mountains terrain I traverse
Both beautiful, horrific feelings and emotions endured
To myself I wonder, *what is time?*

A numeric representation of a point
Displayed in seconds, minutes and hours
Cycled into days, weeks, months, years
Spring, summer, autumn and winter seasons
Broken down by zones across the globe

Time as we know it is now so, enjoy the moment
Time is the present moment, your past dreams in a reality
Time is the independent measure of all existence
A journeyed opportunity to love, share and care
A continuous change that goes beyond infinity

Time is the most constant gift, perceived as an illusion
Time is an equal opportunity for all
Amazingly fair and impartial
The lack thereof to understand, to be understood
Time moves in a straight line; beyond infinity

It cannot be reinvented, rearranged or deleted
Time cannot be borrowed, purchased nor sold
Time cannot be saved or reserved
Fortunately, time is the ever-changing moment
Gracefully, time can be both fair and forgiving

Time never presents itself early or late
It never limits one's potential to be great

Time is slow to the idler but precious to the wise
It's the inspiration that builds and reveals one's potential
Time is the raging fire in which we soar

Consumed by our indulgences and indifferences
Time is the healing habitation in which we love and grow
Entwined by faith provides closure to our wounds
Beyond reasons, for which cannot be explained or changed,
Time coupled with forgiveness heals fears, feelings and emotions

The most valuable and least respected asset is time
Forever, time will constantly remain in motion
Time changes people without altering past images
Time awaits no one
Time well harnessed is the remedy for success

I see time in space and dimensions
Your understanding of time fuels your dreams
Your utilization of time determines your success
Time is immeasurable
Time is the overseer of all things

"

"Time is free but it's priceless. You can't own it, but you can use it. You can't keep it but you can spend it. Once you've lost it you can never get it back."
Harvey Mackay

"

Tomorrow

Tomorrow is a mystery-filled concept
The day of which we speak and dream of
A day that lays in the future; it doesn't exist
It's a mythical destination where success,
Accomplishment, motivation and goals are stored

We worry about tomorrow like it's promised
You can fantasize, envision, and estimate it
But tomorrow, you cannot advance
Not by a second, minute or hour; it never comes early or late
Because nothing can be accomplished until the moment arrives

Tomorrow's predictions aren't guaranteed
Tomorrow holds the unknown
Tomorrow will rise after midnight
Before the break of dawn
Before the darkness yields to the rising sun

Filled with fresh starts, adventures and new beginnings
Joy, peace, grace, success and blessings
Projections and estimates; promises beyond expectations
Potential burdens, trials, defeats and conflicts

So, use the present to develop tomorrow's desires
And encounter tomorrow with today's strength
It's the place where visions become mature
Because tomorrow is the hope where you place your faith

And just like the sunrise,
Tomorrow is waiting on the other side
Tomorrow will be a better day

"

"Do not boast about tomorrow, for you do not know what a day may bring."
Proverbs 1:27

"

Go Traveling

Traveling; the precious privilege to live and evolve
To escape, breathe, explore, enjoy and love
To roam and learn the roads of lands remote
Escape the sadness and brutalities,
Wallow in the joys and beauties of life
See the world; broaden your horizon

Start where you are to change the ending
Place one foot in from the other; trust strangers
Lose sight of the familiarity, comfort of home and friends
Reflect on the tiny place and space you occupy
Rather than going back to change the beginning
While encountering the untold secrets of destinations

Traveling removes one's assumptions of the world
Discover the truth that lies beneath the wrongs
Remove one's prejudice and narrow mindedness
Get lost and be found; understand one's self
Shape your thoughts; see more than you can remember
Remember more than what you can see

Much more than seeing beautiful iconic places
Explore the world's DNA and possibilities
Explore the attractive landscapes
Meet those who share your interests
Make discoveries, explore your inner child
While marveling for excitement in search of fulfillment

We travel to live, learn and grow
Travel to rise above our fears and falls
Navigate our uncertainties and discomforts
Tour the world toward a better future

Travel to heal one's mind, heart and soul
A new way of seeing the world of wonders

We have nothing to lose but a world to see
Focus on what's important, magnify human emotions
Capture the good, strengthen our weaknesses
Answer the questions you only thought of asking
Accomplish a task you may never comprehend
Life's not meant to be lived in on place

Go Travel

"

"The world is a book, and those who do not travel, read only one page."
St. Augustine

"

Wildflower

She isn't just another flower
Grounded, beautiful and full of joy
She needs no restraints
All she needs is the sun in her hair
And the wind in her sail

She's adaptive and versatile
Rooted deep in the rocky gardens
Flourishes in hilly landscapes
A tolerant of porous soil conditions
She thrives and rises above circumstances

She's a flower growing free
She is beautiful and vibrant
From an assorted species
A diverse variety of sizes, and shapes
In season, she exposes her true shades

She celebrates her natural beauty
She blossoms and releases her seeds to the wind
She opens to the warmth of the sunshine
She closes to the dark of the night
Much more than a flower; she is a punctual Nyctinastic

She rejects the creatures of the night
She blossoms and attracts the butterflies and bees
She's a flower among the thorns
Waiting to be plucked
By hands not scared to be pricked

She's the Gazania Daisy
She's the Morning Glory

She's the California Poppy
She's the Lily in the Valley
She's an Orchid, she's a Marigold

Reflection

It's our natural human instinct to try to figure out what we are meant to do in this beautiful life we have been given. However, it is not that obvious because we all know that life often presents unforeseen challenges, which for the most part, take all the fun out of our day-to-day lives. But how can we overcome these obstacles?

There are a lot of good strategies you can employ, and very often, the answer to our greater desire in life lies within. I find joy, peace, and fulfillment in my life when I journal and write poems. I invite you to complete the journaling questions below so, you can create your own happy life, filled with purpose on your terms. Don't forget that the only limit to achieving our desires is one of imagination!

1. **What value have you placed on life?**

2. **What does "living your truth" mean to you?**

3. **What is the difference between you living and just existing?**

4. **When do you feel most like your authentic self?**

5. **Are there any disappointments in your past that you can change for the better tomorrow?**

6. **Have you developed a vision for your future?**

SECTION FIVE

Love & Relationship

*"Love bears all things, believes all things,
hopes all things, endure all things."*
1 Corinthians 13: 7

Love and affection are an individual's feelings of fondness. A desire to be cared for and to be in proximity to the other. The way a person makes you feel mentally and emotionally, aids in the love you will have for each other. When it comes to love, relationships, and dating, the conversations should go beyond the surface in order to get to the heart and soul.

Love and affection are two very important aspects of a relationship because it helps you to experience an enriched sense of love, peace, mutual understanding, and harmony. This is not limited to just physical and sexual intimacy but goes beyond all interactions. The importance of love and affection may vary from person to person depending on an individual's experience, preference, and lifestyle. I invite you to delve right into my heart with the following poems I have penned.

Craving and Moaning

She said, "I am hungry. I am craving for your passion
My soul longs for your touch and submission
Your hands over my wrist; your strength over my softness
Your control over my weaknesses and your need over my desires
Consume me!

I crave for the collision that sets my soul ablaze
Transform my thoughts into delight
Kiss by kiss I need you to cover my tiny infinities
My margins and rivers, my diminutive villages
I fantasize over your exploration of my body

I no longer need your gentle kisses
My body wasn't meant for soft caresses
So, touch me in places without hesitation
Where your lips will soon follow without limitations
Kiss me passionately, without fears, regrets or procrastination

My mind needs your well-executed seduction
My body desires to be aroused and satisfied
So, stimulate me in places where I can feel and cannot see
Let my soul sing with joy of exquisite pleasure
I need to be savagely explored"

She tilts her head backward,
Forcing my lips to her neck, to her breast
Kissing and licking the edges of her forever secrets,
As she moans to my sensitive touch and kisses
She purrs, *"I'm losing it. I want more."*

"Touch me with your fingers full of longing
Perform unspeakable acts of joy, love and pleasure

The things that words cannot describe
The things that make my skin shivers like brail
And make my heart leap into something gruesome."

I remove her laces, spread her thighs
And inhale her sweetness as she trembles
Stroking and igniting her inner flame
Exploring her secrets with a combination
Allowing her lips to taste my naughty imagination

With her fervent screaming and moans
Her legs wrapped around my waist
Digging deeper into my flesh with her nails
Leaving teeth marks of love notes bitten in my flesh
She says,
"My body is your landscape.
I can feel your pulse inside of me."

"

*"Hold and cherish my breast, and derriere
with ferocity. Trace and explore the curves of
my landscape as your exploiting lips taste the
secrets of my being. Unravel my riddles with
your tongue and turn my words into
moans of intelligence."*
Mendez Frith

"

Emotionally Connected

Emotionally connected, physically attracted
Beyond romance, above friendship
Defined over time and through distance—
Forever connected through love

The feeling of delight as we laugh and talk
The passion felt between us when we are together
The existence of you and I, deep in our souls,
Creates an extraordinary happiness that is rear

Our emotions and sensitivity toward each other
Absorbs as we grow together
Capture the opportunities to strengthen one's love
Romantically inter mingle with each-others thoughts

Many times, our phrases lead to assumptions
Other times too many words lead to investigations
Assume nothing but seek clarifications
Be open with each other; be true to each other

Show your moments of understanding and care
Maintain an open mind that deepens your understanding
An emotional connection is not a born trait
It's a learned skill, leading to a deeper emotional union

Allow your intimacy to grow; embrace the feel within
Touch me through your words, share your moments
Be thoughtful in your conversation,
Emotionally connected in love

"

"She craves much more than a physical connection. She craves my fears and desires. She desires an emotional connection beyond the depth of my surface."
Mendez Frith

"

Look @ Me; She Said

I looked in her beautiful eyes
A flickering flame waiting to be kindled
I saw her in her most gorgeous state
She revealed her landscape and most dangerous curves
I looked at her in awe

I looked in a state of shock and unbelief
As her lingerie fell to the floor
With a rising of the pulses
And butterfly jittery stomach
My jaw dropped frozen in the moment

I looked @ her scars and perfect imperfections
She had her own style and class
She had her own made-up mind
I saw the fire in her soul; she was glowing
I looked and saw her naked truth

Her beauty transcends the physical
She gave a look of closeness that isn't about proximity
But belonging
I looked
She was beautiful
You're safe with me

66

"He looked at her the way she needed to be looked at. Like the whole world could crumble and he wouldn't blink."
Atticus

99

Love As a Source

Deeply involved in each other's lives
The patience of each other
Your daily needs and desires
Your love must be the source of sharing

The furies of the storms in your daily lives
The calmness of the moments, seemingly still
The beautiful sight of loving couples
All makes love the source of passion

Having each other's shoulder as a source of refuge
You're special for each other to count on
Regardless of each other's differences
Missing each other across the distances
Been in each other's hearts at all times
Proving that love is the source of security

Freedom to peruse together, your dreams and desires
Sharing your experiences by way of growth
Through personal achievements and accomplishments
Forming unity and togetherness
Love shows the source of success

Two once were apart, now become one
Our understanding and acceptance of each other
Made a unified relationship
The simple things that make togetherness
Your love is the source of unification

Be happy with and for each other
Support each other in anguish
Unification brings togetherness

Both in the difficult and wonderful times
Love is the source of strength

The most beautiful things in life are often unseen
The best things in life cannot be touched
The love that comes from the heart cannot be touched or seen
The love in our hearts will not always be displayed
Instead, our love must be felt in each other's heart

"

"Love starts as a feeling, but to continue is a choice. And I find myself choosing you, more and more every day."
Justin Wetch

"

My Soul

Deep within my heart lies my soul
That reflects through my eyes
Whispers through my lips
My true feelings and emotions

My soul bears the scars of my life
As they reflect how far I have come
My soul brings forth my dreams
As it sees my journey ahead

Unfold my soul and you will find strength
Bravery, faith, love warmth and comfort
Happiness, blessings, joy and humility
My soul comes from the Lord who guides me

66

"Fall in love with my soul before you fall in love with my body."
Mendez Frith

99

Naked

Naked, her silhouetted temple stood vulnerable
Her heart, mind and soul revealed on her radiant facial expression
Baring her thoughts, ideas, hopes, dreams and visions
She introduced me to her strengths and weaknesses
And walked me along her past journeys and setbacks
Nothing she left to the imagination

She exposed her emotions and inner spirit
Her vulnerabilities, mysteries, every scar, every secret
Her joyous smiles, tears and fears of today
Past memories and worries of tomorrow
She has been hurt, bruised, broken, betrayed and rejected
She was naked

She endured pains, dealt with drama
She withstood the fire and raging storms
Overcame the deceit far beyond the norms
So away I wiped her sacred tears
Removed the doubts and fears
Intimately naked to the touch

With my eyes open, her open heart she entrusted me
She removed the scales and veils from my eyes
Expelled many thoughts, doubts or misconceptions
Allowed me to see much deeper than the natural sight
The invisible that can only be seen with the art of a vision
I saw her optimism, aspirations and dreams

There was beauty in her brokenness
I opened my arms and hugged her nakedness
She crawled under the protection of my umbrella
Where she never felt such luxury of safety

Understanding, fortification and comfort,
She was naked

I claimed her; I made her mine
I became her inner strength
She became my inner weakness
She was no longer naked
She was covered and protected

"

*"Show me the most damaged parts of your soul,
and I will show you how it still shines like gold."*
Nikita Gill

"

Shared Affection

Our first sight of attraction drew us together
Endearing and unique qualities we found in each other
Our love kindled and strengthened together
Two individuals joined and became one
A unique connection; a loving couple

I met you
I found my wife
As companions, we share our joys
As friends we lift our burdens
On your shoulder is where I found comfort
In you I can always confide

We have the passion that bonds together
A person of endless pleasure
A lifetime of memories to treasure
Our journey filled with companionship
A lifetime source of friendship

Years spent together so many memories made
Our eternal affection and admiration grew
Our relationship firmly strengthened
An unassailable bond made our marriage secure
Makes this anniversary special

“

"We're all a little weird, and life's a little weird. And when we find someone, whose weirdness is compatible with ours, we join up with them and fall in mutual weirdness and call it love."
Dr. Seuss

”

Souls Collide

I forged mountain ranges and oceans
I forged the fixed fortifications
Obstacles and monuments of man's stupidity
Overcoming fear, discomfort and uncertainty
To meet you on the edges of forever
Where missing pieces of our souls found each other

You gave me your body, mind and devotion
You gave me your respect and heart
You gave your gratitude
You revealed yourself to me
Through obedience, you gave me your all
With me you shared your deepest secrets

Without fear you loved from your heart
You asked without demanding
You trust without questioning
You gave access without restrictions
You accepted my past and support my present
You encourage my future

Through your mind, I entered to win your body
With an overwhelming urge I protect you
So, I treasure your heart after it's been won
Your happiness became my duty
Caring for you became my assignment
And loving you—my life

We accepted each other's imperfections
We cast away our shores and borders
Entwined our souls together
For a deepening growth and surrender

For the beauty, unity and creativity
Of love and grace within our hearts

Your love came without a notification
You had my heart before I could say no
In a sky of stars my eyes will always search for you
True love has been the greatest adventure
Since our Soul's collided

"

"*Our eyes intersected, our heart and soul connected, our minds intertwined! Ever since, nothing has kept us apart.*"
Mendez Frith

"

That Woman

You are much more than a pretty face
Your scars decorate and reveal your true beauty
You fight without sympathy
You're a warrior and a courageous fighter
You're a daughter, a sister and a mother
You mastered the combination of strength and power

You've been betrayed, broken and rejected
You've cried tears; yet you continued to smile
You remain proud, humble and fearless
You forgo revenge and rose stronger than a victim
Firmly standing with honor and love

You have the fire that burns within one's soul
You house the thunder that rolls within your heart
You carry the storms within your veins
You bring sunshine and life after the storms
So never underestimate your own power
Because you're not limited by one's imagination

You are confident and know your worth
No comparison between yourself and others
You are a lady with such style, grace and class
You have standards with established boundaries
You have a mind, and an attitude of your own
You're an incredible and worthy human being

You are uniquely created
Filled with substance and honesty
Impeccable character and integrity
You value respect, love, trust and loyalty

Compassion, elegance, strength and empathy
You are imperfect but beautiful

Your lips have kissed shame
You sipped the game called blame
You nibbled at your regrets
You swallowed your pride
Your soul has tasted heartaches
But nothing as the flavor of integrity

You are educated and dedicated
You crave a love that's evolved
You have a heart filled with love
Ears readily available to listen
And hands willing to help
You're a problem solver

You are authentic and aggressive
You stimulate the mind, body and soul
Your light shines through darkness
You turned rejection into direction
And become a pathfinder and trail blazer
You're a pace setter and a constant shining star

You are that woman!

"Through each and every changing season, you speak with a voice of reason. Without boundaries you diminish darkness; like a star you continuously shine, illuminating those within your heavens much brighter than you'll ever know."
Mendez Frith

The Essence of Your Landscape

From the lit fireplace, your silhouette casts a shadow
Your enclosed heart wrapped in smooth velvet
The burning candle lights reveal your essence
Your strawberry lips yearning for my kisses
As your outreach hands await my touch

Allow me to embrace and caress you
Feel your rising pulses through sensual kisses
Fading softly across your tender skin
Tasting the glands of your sweet and tender lips

With my fingers grazing across your frame
Destined to please and satisfy
Inch by inch, I make love to your body
Cupping, caressing and nibbling on your breast

Whispering fantasies and desires
Inspiring dreams that dazzles through your mind
Fusing thoughts and actions, sparking an internal fire
As your body thrusts against mine

To my rhythm, you groove and moan above the silence
As syllables and phrases flow from your soul to your lips
Speaking in tongues, reaching a erotic high with every breath
Releasing warm and sweet caramel honey
As your nails rake my back in sheer delight

Forgive my tongue as it tastes your landscape
Knowing every touch of my lips making you tremble
While my fingertips play your fantasies like an instrument
Touching your mind while liquefying your flesh
Leaving you craving for more

"

"*Let me navigate your sculptured thighs to places less traveled. With my lips I taste the sweet essence of your flavor, satisfying your every desire.*"
Mendez Frith

"

The Poet

Like an open novel, I read your body language
Captivated by the tiny flame flickering in your eyes
Yearning my control and ignition of your smoldering desire
Skin wrapped with passion and smiles
Your soul and emotions shining from within

Swept away amid your pages and thoughts
Intoxicated by the throbbing lyric that flows from my lips
She winked and gave me that carnal look
Wanting to indulge in the most decadent ways
I fantasize over your mind and body

Reveal to me your passions, hidden secrets and desires
Reveal your temptations and imaginations
Allow me to seduce and undress your soul
Savor the sweetness of your breasts, compose your sexual submissions

With my fingers, I tickle and tease; excite and please
Exploring and enjoying your every curve
Playing instruments and writing poetry between your thighs
Your skin, like braille, shivers waiting to be read

My lips walk wild across your skin
Exploring and discovering, tasting the secrets of your being
In silence writing syllables of my hopes and dreams
To the depth and boundaries of your willpower
Tasting your darkest and sexual desires

Free your mind; release your spontaneities
Expose your wild temptations
Allow me to go down on your thoughts

Taste your imaginations and perceptions
Giving you multiple intellectual orgasms

My fingers, lips and tongue are writing tools
To compose poetry on your breast
Prose on your stomach
And chapter my greatest novel between your thighs
As your nails engrave love notes on my back

I want to touch the edges of your obscure soul
Kiss the pieces of your being that's most secret
Kiss the pieces hidden from the world
Igniting your flame of passion
Let me be your poet

"

"She is a loving deer, a graceful doe.
Let her breasts satisfy you always.
May you always be captivated by her love."
Proverbs 5:19

"

Tongue Kisses

The feeling of lips fusing together as one
Housing the messenger that run errands of the heart
That signal a language without being spoken
Where caresses and kisses reveal one's passion
Telling stories as two stars collide
Kisses; the pure and raw form of intimate contact

Allow me to kiss you to the beat of your heart
Enlighten you with the passion of my unspoken words
With kisses that elevates the pounding of your heart
Kisses that make your skin tingle
Seducing and conquering your mental barriers
While keeping your heart safe in the warmth of my arms

Close your eyes; as I place my hands upon your breast
Let the rhythm of my lips speak softly what you've longed for
Let my kisses speak without echoing a single syllable
As you feel my every unspoken word; unhinged!
Your heart pulsates with your every breath calling out my name

As syllables, sounds and gestures flow from your tongue
My kisses discover all the beautiful moments and places
That perfectly fits the shape of my lips
Smearing words upon your flesh
Branding and reminding you that you are being loved

With lips filled with fierce, dominating and intensions of pleasure
Long slow soft tongue kisses that satisfies your desires
Undressing your conscience, assaulting your senses
Allow me to kiss you beyond the edges of your overflow
Leaving nothing to the imagination

Kiss by kiss, I'll cover your insecurities and fancies
Your lingering dents and torn edges of your heart
Crawl inside your mind and run your imaginations wild
Slipping through the channels of your veins
To the precipice of your carnal; until I hear
Those beautiful, magical commanding and powerful words

Lost in a haze of carnal desires
My lips and tongue speak in codes
A language only your body comprehends
Transforming into a delicious torment
As you moan and groan, setting your soul ablaze
Elevating you to the stars, moon and open heavens

With every kiss, you become more unhinged
As your body and lips oblige under my control
I tasted ecstasy

66

"Passionate kisses should never be taken likely. It goes beyond any touch and breathe life into a forgotten soul."
Mendez Frith

99

Who Are You?

Chocolate brown sugar gold complexion
Clothed with maturity, strength and dignity
Body built like a champion
She chooses to maintain a voice of silence
But wears a screaming crown of confidence
Lady, who are you?

I saw you peeping and looking my way
Eyeing me as I go about my day
Your sparkling eyes scanned me like an x-ray
Strawberry colored lips that stole my words away
Beautiful, to whom do I have the privilege of speaking to?

I'm a lady.
Intelligent, innovative, independent, influential
Courageous, captivating, sensual, sensational,
Grounded, fearless, unapologetic, brilliant
Made whole!
Unique, talented, and resilient
Beautiful, powerful, loving and elegant

I am bold and empowered
I've towered over my circumstances
I am a beautiful piece of broken pottery
Beautifully placed back together
I've been awaiting your approach
What took you so long to ask my name?

"

*"I am a temple and a vessel of divine light.
I style things my way. I am a proud
and humble queen."*
Mendez Frith

"

Your Presence

As flawed as we both are
As unattractive as we sometimes feel
As unaccomplished as we may think we are
I love you just as you are
Your presence illuminates my soul

Your love I have never experienced so clear
So pure and refined is the love that we share
My heart skips a beat when I'm in your presence
My soul smiles each time I lay next to you
What joy I feel when I am next to you

You're there for me and I'm there for you
Together and forever, we will grow
Until the end of time, I'll be next to you
Until the sun, moon and stars are lost in our lives
Until the earth and heavens are combined
I'll always love you

Our heart defines what we share
Our soul determines our destiny
Together as one, our minds are entwined
Together our thoughts are combined
For each other we were designed
In my heart you are always present

"

"The most precious gift you can give to the one you love is your time, presence and attention."
Mendez Frith

"

Reflection

Having a healthy relationship is essential to our being. We all have someone whom we care for deeply and want to have around us. We also have those who we struggle with. I have provided you with a few love, and relationship journal prompts. They are designed to help you honor your space of being a better person to your loved ones. This is the space for you to examine your relationships so you can know what steps you need to take to improve your relationships if needed. In the end, the quality of your relationships hinges on you and how you show up.

1. Have you ever been in love?

2. Are you an adventurous lover?

3. Are you committed to co-creating a relationship?

4. In what ways would you like to see your relationship grow

   in intimacy?

5. Are you the same person in all of your relationships?

   Why or why not?

6. Are you giving or getting more from your relationships right now?

SECTION SIX

Finding Resiliency in The War of Life

"No matter how much falls on us, we keep plowing ahead.
That's the only way to keep the roads clear."
– Greg Kincaid

These poems of inspirations are based on real life experiences, challenges, views, and obstacles that I faced during the wars in Iraq and Afghanistan as a Soldier. I am expected to be resilient; develop a mental, physical, emotional, and behavioral ability to face and cope with adversity, adapt to change, learn, recover, and grow from setbacks. Building resiliency requires the recognition that everyone is unique and will react differently to stressors. Building resiliency warrants a holistic approach for development.

It's a gentle reminder that my resiliency has allowed me to overcome so many obstacles. Dusting myself off, putting myself back together... with the help of others too and driving on with life's challenges. Enjoy!

Concrete Jungle

A country scarred by decades of conflicts and never-ending wars
A city ravished, destroyed by corruption and political bureaucracies of war
Imprisoned are the innocent
Crumbled are their voices and stories, goals, aspirations, hopes and dreams
Dismantled, trapped under the rubbles and craters so no one knows
Constrained by the strewn T-Walls erected by the coalition

A city, a network of walls and sentry towers made of concrete
Neighborhoods littered with checkpoints, roads blocks, and razor wire
fences
Streets cluttered with hopeless and desperate bodies
Entangling civilization while forming a human zoo
Monitoring every step and movements made

Families marred by the tragedies and demons of war
Burdened by the human losses and suffering of war
The heavy weight of a city displays on their faces
The sighs and distress heard in their voices
And expressed by tear drops rolling down their cheeks

Life seems to have lost its meaning
Like the sun and the moon, their once brilliant light now gloomy and
unseeing
The neighborhood kids can no longer come out to play
Their playgrounds filled with craters, barriers of concrete and scrap metal
hay
Lost are their voices of triumph and dignity, as they're barricaded in
captivity
As their itinerary tangle among the destruction of humanity

Concrete; erected under the cover of darkness
Trapping lives, treasure, blood, sweat and tears

Choking off access to basic services, necessities and goods
Leaving residents to become prisoners in their neighborhood
As communities struggle to see a common good

The challenges of a curfew, chaos and daily humiliation
No freedom, no commodities or social occasions
No justice, no morality, no escape for the weary
Where should the children come out and play
When their doors and windows open to a concrete jungle

"

"No chains around my feet but I'm not free, oh-oh. I know I am bound here in captivity."
Bob Marley

"

Children; The Faces of The Syrian War

Born in the midst of the Syrian civil war
Where over 300,000 innocent lives lost
Over 4,500 children dismantled, laid victims
Millions displaced from their residence without hope
The images of victimized children tell the story
Bearing the burden of a war-torn country

Startling images, symbols of despair, distressed
Bewildered, weary, astonished and shocked
Face coated with gray dust and encrusted blood
Loss in the chaos and fury is a boy named, Omran
Channeling the devastation and crisis
That no human should ever see

Grave violations against children and humanity
Over 300,000 children born as a refugees
Their lives shaped by violence, fear and displacement
Grown into adolescence and adulthood as orphans
Untrained, unemployed, hungry with no opportunity
An entire uneducated generation lost to a civil war

With the lack of peace, families displaced as refugees
Facing daily challenges, Children living in besiege
Toddlers drowning, bodies washed ashore
Not for the lack of parental love and care
Numbed to the ongoing disasters
That shines the light on the harrowing carnages

Children receiving military training; maintaining weapons
Many serving in combat; performing life threatening roles
Manning check points across the battlefield
Children used as killers; in many cases execution style
While some are treating and evacuating the wounded
Many burying the dead

A country convulsed by depression and conflict
Indescribable and harrowing attacks
Gruesome bodies lay under rubbles
Lifeless bodies in the streets
As war planes patrol the skies during the hours of prayer
While rebels attempt to protect their territories

An uprising against an oppressing ruler
Mushroomed into a brutal proxy war
A war consisting of regional and world powers
Bombs, artillery, and rockets fall through the unfriendly skies
Demolishing neighborhoods, with every strike
As unwilling global powers failed to intervene

"

"For a warrior, it is not enough to win a war. It is more important to organize the peace."
Aristotle

"

Fire Mission

It was us against the insurgency
In a society filled with terror and deadly weaponry
Suicides, bombs, guns, and snipers
An enemy determined to surmount a coup

Locked in the middle of a war, rolling up and down the 95
Me and my crew rolling through the desert in my M109
On patrol are the friendly troops in contact
With their backs against the wall
A fire for effect is their requested call

FIRE MISSION; at my command
Red-One, Six Rounds, Shell HE-RAP, fuze quick
Charge 8, deflection 3852; quadrant 756. Fire!
A barrage of 155mm pierces and whistles through the air
From day light through the dark of the night
The sound of artillery roars loud and clear
Load another one!

Filled with hate, venom and corruption are my enemy's hearts
Alley ways, bypasses, bridges, highways and arteries
Open desert and trails all became the demise trap of the enemy
Splash!
When the dust and smoke clear all movement cease
As bodies laid unrecognized, dismantled and splattered

From Tikrit to patrol bases in Samarra
To my comrades bunkered down in Palliwada
The earth shakes from curtains of torrential precision artillery strikes
As explosions rumble and thunders across the far distance
While shrapnel rains a trail of destruction to the human souls
As fire balls and black smoke rises and shadows the skies
Repeat!

"

"If you're going through hell, keep going."
Winston Churchill

"

I Am an American Soldier

From the countryside of Jamaica
To the beautiful States of America
I've travelled the European countries
Across the deserts of the Middle East
Through the mountains of Afghanistan
The secured borders of the Korean Peninsula
And other far reaches across this earth

I've trained Leaders, Soldiers and Paratroopers
Influenced the lives of thousands
I've been in the presence of royalties
I've kept the company of dignitaries
Witnessed great beauty in the making
Impacted the operations of cities
But in my mind, I'm no saint

I fought on the frontlines with my comrades
Patrolled the streets of Baghdad
Kicked in the doors of my foes
Fought the Taliban in Afghanistan
Stared in the faces of death and destruction
I've witnessed the strong and courageous
I've overcome dangers and adversities

I've wandered and roamed the cities
Had visions and dreams of a better world
Provided humanitarian assistance to the weak
Altered the thoughts and actions of many

Deleted the lives of my enemies
My fears, I have conquered
To find myself right where I belong

Between my shoulders I bear the weight of my country
I wear the uniform of the brave
I travelled places where many men not dare
I saw things no human should ever bear
I have visions that will forever remain unclear
On my right sleeve I wear the American flag
RED, WHITE and BLUE

So place your feet in my shoes
Take a walk down my path
Come take a glimpse from my views
And hear a few of my thoughts
See my scars and wounds of battles
So, you know where lays my heart

On my journey I pray for peace
My journey is my adventure
My adventure tells my story
My journey forms my connecting tissues
I am the thread, the seams and fabric of humanity
Who pays the price and debts of FREEDOM
I am an American Soldier

"

"The United States has sent many of its fine young men and women into the great peril to fight for freedom beyond our borders."
Colin Powell

"

Incoming

The whistles of indirect fired rounds shattered my midday nap
A Soldier yelled, "Incoming! Take cover!"
Rounds coming from places we couldn't see
But captured by the eyes of the friendly fire finder
Those bastards had zero chance of survival

A heavy thud followed by a heavy explosion
Combined with a sound similar to lightning and thunder
Pieces of shrapnel fly piercing through the air
Searing off anything in its path

The shell shock of an attack
I heard the unseen dismantled shrapnel whizzed me by
I felt as if I could smack them out of the air like a buzzing fly
But how can I see such deadly object whizzing at such speed?
That's the moment I realized I could have been perished

I ran as fast as I could through the lead rain
My heart pumped adrenalin through my veins
"Medic. Someone, grab a stretcher!"

Splashed by the blood of my comrades
Baptized under enemy fire
Brave and fearless, we faced it all

66

"A hissing screaming squall of incoming enemy fire unto our friendly position. Someone yelled, incoming: take cover."
Mendez Frith

99

Isolated Scars

Missions executed by those who volunteer
Answering the nations call is the American Soldier
Across distant lands torn by wars
Enduring brutality and emotional isolation
Challenging one's spirits deep within

Harsh realities too many times revealed
Explosions, indirect fire and gun shots echoes
Vehicles blown apart by EFPs as lives shred
My heart aches as my comrade's life fades
From images seen through the eyes of the beholder
Only a few will ever know the stories untold

Father, guide us because we know you care
Allow our broken hearts to heal through our tears
May the pouring rain wash our sins away
Relieve us from the pain we face each day
As our father forgives our scars and mistakes

A healthy return home is a Soldier's desire
Many dealt a physical and mental blow, too many lives slain
Home tensions, recurring war memories
Shown through the emotional or psychological worries
Irritable, anxiety and sleeplessness; PTSD emerges

Stand up America, let the healing begin
For many who served the mission is still ongoing
Our invisible wounds go undetected
More like our untold stories go unheard
Laying in isolation with the remnants and the demons of war

Our wounds are devastating
Invisible and life threatening
Our stories are real and unforgettable

"It is no longer the contusions across my body that hurts. It is the gashes of the heart and the scars in my mind."
Mendez Frith

It Wasn't My Time

From behind the tempered ballistics
I witnessed the blast in slow motion
The rippling waves of energy from the explosion
Tossed the hummer into a spin

Dirt, gravel, and shrapnel blasted everywhere
A damaged engine with fluids spilled everywhere
Shattered glass, busted tire
The smoke and dust filled the air

I was shocked though; I saw things clear
I was enraged but, I had no fear
We reacted just as we trained and rehearsed
We jumped into action to save my men

Despite the long hours and hundreds of patrols
Despite the gunshots and fire fights
The near missed IED blasts and ambushes
It wasn't my time

I will never know how many IED's attacks I escaped
Some buried deep at the base of light poles and guard rails
Some concealed and detonated by pressure plates
Some detonated after I went back through gate

Maybe it's the fog and dust of war
It was the hand of God who covered me thus far

"

"No matter how much falls on us, we keep plowing ahead. That's the only way to keep the roads clear."
– Greg Kincaid

"

Lurking In the Shadows

Alone in the distance, he's lurking in the shadow
Hundreds of yards away, I just don't know
One by one, the sniper took aim at us
Many didn't hear the rifling shot
As he waits to see my comrades' take their final breath

He took aim at my battle with a double shot
Attempted to pierce the tempered ballistic glass
Anticipating that he would crumble and fall
Hoping that the flash wouldn't show

He's lying in the shadows hiding and plotting
His tool is a mere piece of metal
With a handle grip, a trigger and a visionary scope
Patrolling these streets on a daily gets harder to cope
Yet I remain optimistic knowing it's not all in my mental

I sense his presence but I cannot see him
On steady alert my eyes open wide with fright
In my mind he follows me like a shadow

I will never know how many times I crossed his scope
But for many reasons he refrained from pulling the trigger
And allowed me to patrol the battlefield-much longer
For that unaware kindness thanks to that unknown sniper

Known for laying souls to bed
Now there's a bounty placed upon his head
As he remains lurking in the shadows

"

"*So complex is the human spirit that it can itself scarce discern the deep springs which impel it to action.*"
Arthur Conan Doyle

"

My Prayer as a Soldier

As I stand here on the battle field
I take a knee asking my Lord PLEASE
Protect me from the hands of my enemy
Lord, save me by thy grace
Save me with thy mercy

As the burdens of our nation leans on our shoulders
I ask for your strength to carry on
With a trembling heart, the mission rolls on
Through battles I lead my young and innocent men
Straight to the heals where my enemies stand

As the days and nights become lengthy
The thoughts and memories become much to bear
I pray you keep me focused on my journey
Protect and shield the lives of the innocent
Convict my enemies for all the pain and strife

For all my fallen comrade: you are not forgotten
I pray they made peace with you, their maker
I pray they made peace while here on earth
Watch over their souls as they lay to rest
And let your eternal love be their guide

Help me to remain faithful to you, Lord
As I seek the path rarely travelled
Forgive me for all my wrong doings
As I knowingly acknowledge my flesh is weak
And that my heart is filled with convictions
Lord, please grant me the courage to seek confession

A symbol of moral obligation
The uniform of duty and tradition
The beliefs for which my country stands
The freedom of my people is what I defend
Risking my life for the future
My life to which the future is bestowed

"

"I love the Lord, for he heard my voice; he heard my cry for mercy. Because he turned his ear to me, I will call on him as long as I live."
Psalm 116: 1-2

"

Silky Wings

1250 Feet AGL 64 paratroopers stand
Travelling the corridors of space
Feeling the bumps, and curves the air displaced
Who wants to jump?
The unfriendly skies ahead, we all fear

My static line in one hand
Forehead damp, knees weakened
Heart pumping, stomach knotting, nerves frayed
With fear of the unforgiving sky my soul is soaked

Airborne @ 130 knots, the plane slows and sways
A steady stare out the opening doors
As 13 knot winds cyclone the air
A person of loyalty, selfless service, integrity, fortitude
And personal courage, my own question I answered

With the best of men, I troop the skies above
To the cable line above I am anchored
Standing in the open door, looking out at the heavens
As the unforgiving sky awaits my entrance

On comes the green light; up 12 out 36 I vigorously exit
Counting from 1 to 6 thousand; I feel the opening shock
My pack tray opens unfolding silky wings
Through the dark and open skies here I come
Earthbound as I drift and slip the open heavens

I feel freedom in the open blues
Floating through corridors of space
Harnessed by silky wings
Airborne; Jump Master!

"

"I am an Airborne trooper! I jump by parachute from any plane in flight. I volunteered to do it, knowing full well the hazards of my choice." **Airborne Creed.**

"

Silky Wings II

Green Light Go!
I vigorously exit into the fathomless heavens
With a gut wrenching feel of the unknown
Thrown by the thrust and gusts of the jets
Consumed by jittery and adrenalin blasts
Plummeting to the precipice of earth

Tucked and falling at unimaginable speeds
I hear the snapping of the retention bands
Releasing my static line; unseating the main curved pin
Triggering the deployment sequence of my Canopy
As I count the seconds for my wings to unfold

I reach up and secure my risers
Checking and gaining canopy control
Looking to my left, right and the unknown
Avoiding all jumpers and hazards
Descending to the approaching the ground

The high-pitched sounds of the jet engines fade
I inhale the distinct scent of the exhaust
While it increases its speed in the distance
The chattering and laughing of other paratroopers
Breaking the silence of the air

Flying amongst the white and fluffy clouds
Absorbing the fullness and quiet of the air
The refreshing taste and smell of the unknown
Observing the varied shades of vegetation below
The tranquility of being an airborne Soldier

At about 200ft above the surface; I lowered my equipment
Slipped into the wind and prepared to land
My eyes on the horizon; chin and elbows tucked
My feet and knees together; knees slightly bent
Awaiting the impact of the approaching ground

I land on the balls of my feet
Rolled on my exposed body
As my calf's, thighs, buttocks and
Pull-up muscles embrace the impact
I activate my canopy release assembly

Completing my last point of performance
I take a moment or two to gather myself
Remove my parachute harness
Recover my silky wings
From traveling the open heavens

My own question, I answered.
I must have lost my mind!

"

"That which does not kill us makes us stronger."
Friedrich Nietzsche

"

Jumping in the White and Fluffy Clouds

Cruising through the darkness of the night skies
I stand dancing and swaying with silky wings
Traveling the fluffy corridors of the dark
From the white bright to tinted blue lights

I hear the wind hissing and whistling
As the seals of left and right trooper doors roll
Opening up to the ceiling highs
As thunderous roaring sounds cyclone the air

Sneaking in comes the bright, white and fluffy clouds
Forming a landscape of foggy mist
Floating between every crevasse and trooper
Leaving no dew, no interference, no obstacles

As the green light illuminates
One by one, we disappeared by jumping
Into the open, dense, white, and fluffy clouds
Littered with silky wings; disturbed by chatty troopers

Snow-like fluffy clouds in heavenly splendor glides by
Roaming at will, floating the unforgiven sky
They form, they storm, and they journey
On angel wings, as I pass them by

It was every where
It obstructed my vision
Of my silky wings harnessed above
Neither could I compare my descent with anyone

The white, dense, fluffy, and weightless clouds
Shielding the rays of the moonlight
Illuminated by the piercing C17 lights
Displacing the energy and fading sounds
As I descended the unforgiving skies

"

"It was everywhere. I could see it; I couldn't touch it, I could inhale it. I couldn't taste it, neither could I smell it. I couldn't hold it, chase it or capture it."
Mendez Frith

"

The Stars and Stripes!

The sacred emblem of my country
The symbol of freedom
I was created in freedom
I am the symbol of your heritage

Red embodies hardiness and valor
White signifies purity and innocence
Blue denotes vigilance, perseverance and justice
Thirteen alternating red and white stripes
Symbolizes the 13 original colonies
Fifty white stars represents the fifty states of the union

A prominent icon in American history
Flown daily is the stars and stripes
Across the landscape of the United States
Raised before the hour of sunrise
Lowered before the hour of sunset
Properly illuminated during hours of darkness

The stars and stripes! Red, white and blue
Flowing in the wind
Billowing on top of the white house to state capitals
From the Pentagon, military installations and memorials
From battlefields, airplane tails, Navy ships and submarines
Sailing over both land and seas

From space ships and satellites to the moon
From churches to schools and homes
Post offices and mailboxes
Police and fire stations
The symbol of hope and unification
Equality and cherished American values

Our flag flies but not by the wind
Our flag flies by the breath
Blood, sweat, tears and sorrows
Of every Soldier, Airman, Marine, Sailor and Coastguards
Who serve securing our liberties
Or died in defense of our freedom

The sacred emblem of heritage and liberty
The symbol of strength and freedom
Perseverance and endurance
Demonstrating unity and pride
To honor and recognize those who have served
In remembrance of those who fought and died

I've worn the red, white and blue
On my right shoulder sleeve
On my hats, ties and pins
I proudly serve to protect and defend
The freedom for which it stands
In honor I'll forever render my salute
The stars and stripes

"

"*You don't burn it, you don't walk on it, and you don't let it touch the ground.*"
Unknown author

"

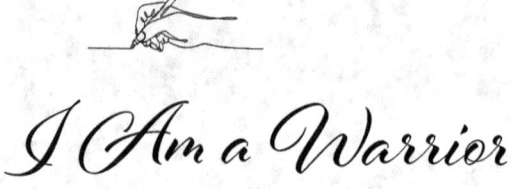

I Am a Warrior

Born in a world filled with insanity and immoralities
Raised in a home filled with love and happiness
Sought the glamour I never had

I overcame the struggles of the night
Enjoyed the fame that came with the light
I survived the pain of hatred and envy

Driven and strayed by the grieves and obstacles in life
I've been through many nightmares and strife
They often had me scared but prepared for life

I've been knocked down but not out
Travelled the streets where many men fear
Places where the lives of men have decayed
Where many former comrades have been slayed
Through it all I've survived

Ignored, victimized and ridiculed, I lived and fought alone
Overcame my fears, mistakes and challenges
Gained strength from my weaknesses

I became fearless because I was afraid
Became wiser because I was a fool
And moved forward with hope

I've been betrayed by the smiles of veiling faces
But through the obstacles in different places
And grounded in my beliefs, I stand firm

Through the journey and turbulences of life
Bruises, discomforts, wounds and strife
I breath the breath of survival

66

"Patiently, I waited. In silence, I suffered. In the shadows, I prepared. Quietly, I endured. I survived in the midst of hopelessness."
Mendez Frith

99

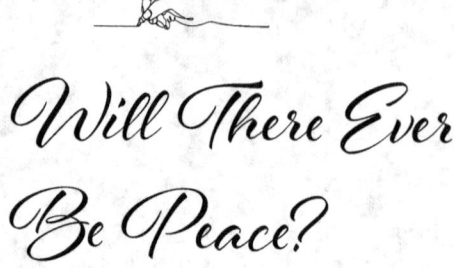

Will There Ever Be Peace?

Our beautiful world is at risk
Serious and deteriorating situations increase across the globe
Joyous world developments are relegated to second place
As states falter, war outbreaks, violence erupts and increase
Governments, extremist groups violate and sanitize the human populous
Will there ever be PEACE?

Regions characterized by conflicts, instability, and hostility
Political, racial and religious in-differences, nations fighting against nations
Convulsed by armed violence, massacres, savagery and mass destruction
Overly consumed by hatred, lack of hope of a free and democratic state
As their actions, ways and lifestyle got them stuck in the past
Will there ever be PEACE?

From an era of dictatorship to an era of extremist fundamentalism
Land grabbing, cage burning, barbaric acts, slashing humanity apart
World leaders have tried to negotiate a lasting PEACE
However, with many and great intentions, nations attempt have failed
To the oppressed citizens the question remains
Will there ever be PEACE?

Deep in their hearts, there's no love for humanity
Many casualties both young and old
Kids being robbed of their childhood; becoming child soldiers
Murdered, raped, gassed; kids robbed of their innocence
With you and I, becoming victims of wars, I wonder
Will there ever be PEACE?

Across our global community we fight for PEACE
Bringing calm and stability to Africa, Europe and the Middle East
Under our country's quest for PEACE, we feel the pressure
How long will this last? In my sleep, I dream of a better future
As I trod the path less traveled, I wonder
Will there ever be PEACE?

On foreign soil, I shed my sweat and tears in search for PEACE
Warplanes patrol the unfriendly skies above
Rockets, cannon artillery aimed at each other
To bombs and guns my comrades have lost their lives
No cries for mercy from the shock and pain they felt
This type of living isn't fun, I uttered as I knelt
Will there ever be PEACE?

In life everything has its time
In life we all must recognize the time
Do we want PEACE in our hearts and mind?
Do we want PEACE across our world?
When the power of love exceeds the love of power
The world will see and know PEACE
In our Lord Jesus Christ, we will find PEACE

Allow the wind to blow storms of love and PEACE across the world
Allow the clouds to bring showers of love and PEACE across the world
Allow the sun to shine the blessings of PEACE amongst our people
Allow PEACE and happiness to breed and reign in the hearts of our people
Why glory in human suffering when we can glory in love and PEACE?
Let's have PEACE with God through our Lord Jesus Christ

"

"*Peace is not the pistol we carry in the streets. Peace is something we mutually seek. Peace is something we make and share. Peace is the value we place on humanity.*"
Mendez Frith

"

Reflection

As a reader, you may be battling with some of these similar situations that I have written about in my poems, or you may be an overcomer. Resilience is a key life skill that everyone should have. It helps you to navigate difficult situations, and setbacks which are a part of life. This compilation of resilience journal questions below will help you to have a better perspective on handling challenges.

1. What areas in your daily living have you struggled with?

2. What mechanisms have you incorporated / developed to overcome the daily stressors in your life?

3. Have you ever been in a position where you were able to mitigate the impacts of mental health through your approach?

4. Have you ever faced an obstacle in your life and overcame it?

5. What traits make you good at what you do?

About the Author

Mendez Frith's life unfolds like a fulfilling story from a "MUST READ" book. Page after page and chapter by chapter tells the story of a man with perseverance, determination, purpose, and influence. Mendez possesses strong faith in God and is firm in his convictions and selfless in his deeds and desires to serve. Mendez aims to live his best life now to the fullest and boldness of his ability.

Mendez is originally from Manchester, Jamaica but migrated to the United States in 1993. He lives in North Carolina with his wife and three children. Having a deep desire to grow professionally, Mendez saw the patriotic opportunity to serve in the U.S. Army. As a military veteran, he has been doing so for over 26 years. He has served in several

European countries with multiple combat tours in Iraq, Afghanistan, and other Middle Eastern countries.

Mendez is the recipient of two Bronze Star Medals, the Defense Meritorious Service Medal, two Meritorious Service Medals, the NATO Medal with a star, the Iraqi Campaign Medal (2 stars), the Afghan Campaign Medal (2 stars), the Global War on Terror Expeditionary Medal and the Global War on Terror Service Medal.

Additionally, Mendez completed the elite Advanced Airborne School (Jumpmaster) and earned the senior-rated (STAR) wings. As a testament to his leadership, Mendez was inducted into the prestigious Sergeant Audie Murphy and Sergeant Morales Clubs. He has a Bachelor's degree in Business Administration and a Master's in National Security Studies.

Poetry is his hobby, a mode of expression, and an outlet that can propel him to rise above himself as his thoughts and ideas breathe and manifest into words; and become an expression of art.

Mendez loves engaging with his readers through social media, which is where he connects with people from different walks of life and can be found on

Linkedin@mendez-frith
Instagram@ mendez_frith
Facebook@ Mendez Frith

Thank you for taking the time to read my book. Your support is greatly appreciated, and I hope you enjoyed it. Please leave a review on Amazon. It would be invaluable to me as an author, and your feedback will assist me in improving and growing as a writer.

Sincerely,

Mendez

www.ingramcontent.com/pod-product-compliance
Lightning Source LLC
Chambersburg PA
CBHW060039150626
46553CB00017BA/567